Making Music

Plucking

Angela Aylmore

 Raintree

Chicago, Illinois

© 2006 Raintree
Published by Raintree, a division of Reed Elsevier, Inc.
Chicago, Illinois
Customer Service 888-363-4266
Visit our website at www.raintreelibrary.com

Printed and bound by South China Printing Company.
10 09 08 07 06
10 9 8 7 6 5 4 3 2 1

Library of Congress Cataloging-in-Publication Data:

Aylmore, Angela.
  Plucking / Angela Aylmore.
      p. cm. -- (Making music)
  Includes index.
  ISBN 1-4109-1606-5 (library binding-hardcover) -- ISBN 1-4109-1611-1
(pbk.) 1. Plucked instruments--Juvenile literature. I. Title. II. Series:
Aylmore, Angela. Making music.
  ML1000.A94 2005
  787'.19--dc22
                                2005002429

Acknowledgments
The publishers would like to thank the following for permission to reproduce photographs:
Alamy pp. **4b**, **5a**, **12**, **17**, **18**; Corbis pp. **4a**, **5b**; Getty Images p. **19** (Photodisc); Harcourt Education pp. **14**, **15** (Gareth Boden); **13** (Debbie Row); **6**, **7**, **8**, **9**, **10a**, **10b**, **11**, **16**, **20**, **21**, **22-23** (Tudor Photography).

Cover photograph of a girl playing a guitar, reproduced with permission of Alamy.

Some words are shown in bold, **like this**. You can find out what they mean by looking in the glossary on page 24.

Contents

Let's Make Music!

We can make **music** by **plucking**!

Nazim plucks his guitar.

bom, bom, bom,

Play the cello.

4

Listen to the lap harp.

Use all of your fingers to play the harp.

Pling, bling

Fingers and Thumbs

Put your finger on the string.
Now **pluck** it!

pluck

Move your fingers quickly. How fast can they go?

pluck
pluck
pluck
pluck
pluck

Pluck the Guitar

Can you play
the guitar?

Pluck it gently.
Make a soft note.

Pluck it hard.
Make a loud note.

9

Big and Small

Listen to the big cello.

Up Tall or Down Flat

This harp stands up tall.

I sit next to it to play it.

This harp lies down flat.

I can play it on my lap.

13

Make Your Own

Can you make an instrument to **pluck**?

Use a box and some rubber bands.

twang-g-g

Pluck the rubber bands
to make a note.

Sounds Like...

Pluck some notes on a violin.

What does it sound like?

Do you think of a dripping faucet?

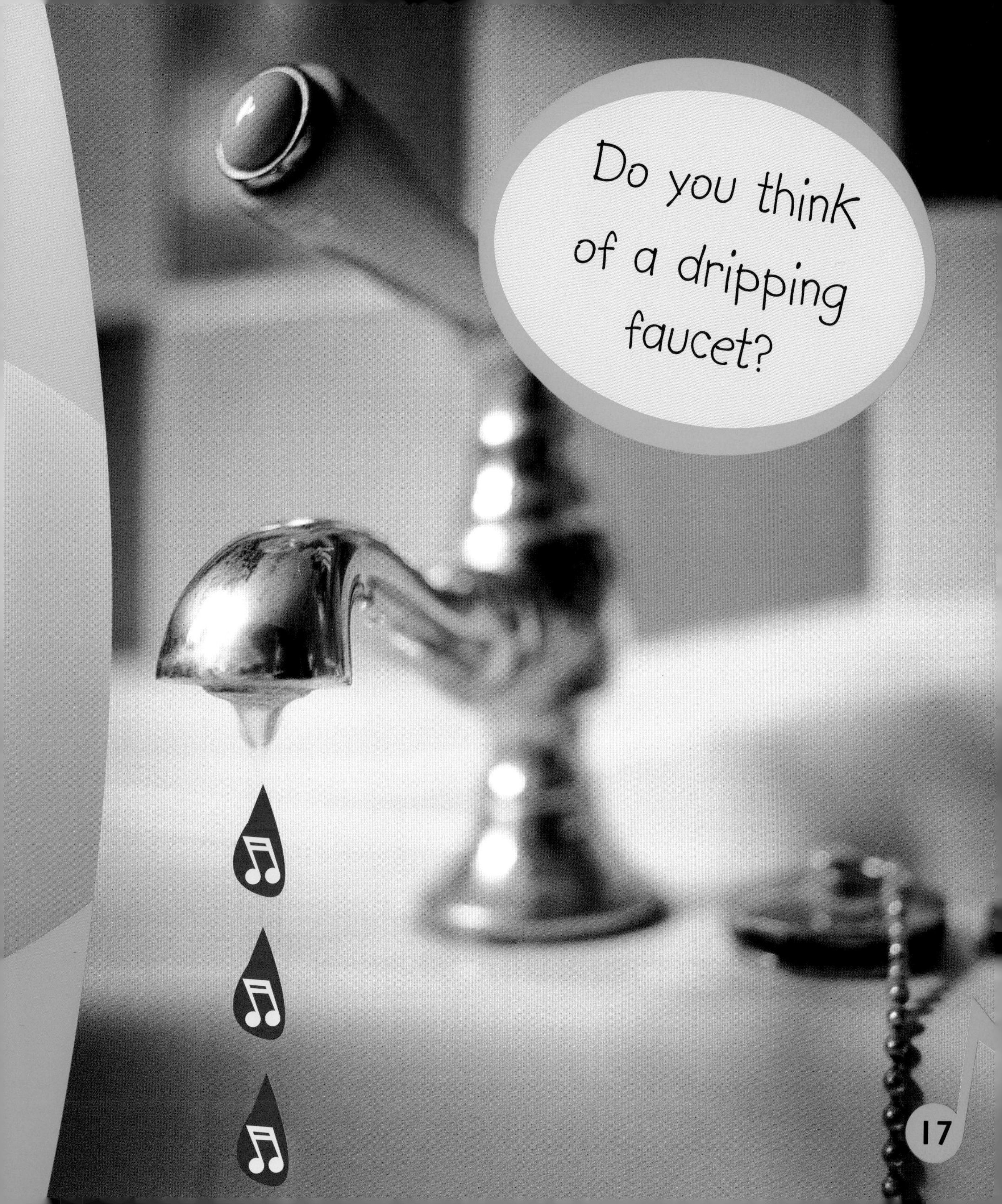

What Is It?

This is a sitar. It comes from India.

This part is round.
It is made from
a pumpkin.

Listen Carefully

What can you hear?
What makes that sound?

violin

maracas

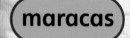

triangle

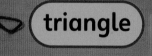

It's the violin!

All Together Now!

pling

pluck

pling

Glossary

listen to pay attention to a sound

music a mixture of sounds to express an idea or emotion

pluck to pull the strings on an instrument and make a sound

Index

Notes for Adults

Making Music provides children with an opportunity to think about sound and the different ways instruments can be played to create music. The concept of volume, rhythm, speed, and pitch are introduced, and children are encouraged to think about how controlling their movements can create different sounds when they play instruments.

This book looks at how to create music by plucking. It looks at different instruments, large and small, that have strings, and the type of sound they make. Plucking is a good way for children to practice control over some fine complex motor-skills, as the book demonstrates how to pluck to make quick, slow, loud, and soft sounds.

Follow-up activities

• Demonstrate to the children how plucking different sized strings on a stringed instrument can produce different notes. Pluck a thick string to produce a low note and a thin string to produce a high note.

• Instruments can be used as links into history. A lyre is an historical stringed instrument, which was used by the ancient Greeks. Show the children pictures of a lyre and ask them if they think it looks like any of the instruments they have seen in this book. What do they think it would have sounded like?